Joe Simon
Creator & Artist

 by Sue Hamilton

Visit us at
www.abdopublishing.com

Published by ABDO Publishing Company, 4940 Viking Drive, Suite 622, Edina, Minnesota 55435.
Copyright ©2007 by Abdo Consulting Group, Inc. International copyrights reserved in all countries.
No part of this book may be reproduced in any form without written permission from the publisher.
ABDO & Daughters™ is a trademark and logo of ABDO Publishing Company.

Printed in the United States.

Editor: John Hamilton
Graphic Design: Sue Hamilton
Cover Design: Neil Klinepier
Cover Illustration: Courtesy Joe Simon
Interior Photos and Illustrations: pp 1–32: All Marvel comic book character and cover images used
with permission by Marvel Entertainment, Inc.
Photos of Joe Simon, his family, and artwork, courtesy Joe Simon, pp 1, 4-6, 7, 9-21, 25-29, 31.
p 8 kid reading comic & *Action Comics* #1 cover, Getty Images.
p 22 bulletin board of banned comics, Corbis.
p 23 kids throwing comics in dumpster, AP/Wide World.

Library of Congress Cataloging-in-Publication Data

Hamilton, Sue L., 1959-
  Joe Simon / Sue Hamilton.
     p. cm. -- (Comic book creators)
  Includes bibliographical references and index.
  ISBN-13: 978-1-59928-300-5
  ISBN-10: 1-59928-300-X
  1. Simon, Joe--Juvenile literature. 2. Cartoonists--United States--Biography--Juvenile
literature.
I. Title. II. Series: Hamilton, Sue L., 1959- Comic book creators.

  PN6727.S51576Z63 2006
  741.5092--dc22
  [B]
                              2006015408

Contents

Comic Book Artist, Writer, and Editor

Captain America. The Blue Beetle. Boy Commandos. The Fly. *Sick* magazine. These are just a few of the most popular comic book creations produced by Joe Simon, the amazing artist, writer, and editor.

Joseph Henry Simon was born October 11, 1913, in Rochester, New York, to Harry and Rose Simon, immigrants from England and Russia. His Dad was a tailor, but Joe grew up not wanting to make suits—he wanted to draw.

Joe Simon grew into quite a talented artist. Using his skills, he went to work on the Benjamin Franklin High School newspaper. He also created art for the school yearbook. Using various tones of grey paint, he developed full-page illustrations for each section of the yearbook: Seniors, Sports, Features, Faculty, and Organizations. These beautiful pieces of art were seen by other schools. Two universities asked to use the very same pictures in their yearbooks. However, because they were used in Benjamin Franklin's publication, the school administrators had to decide if the payment belonged to the school or to Joe Simon.

The school administrators voted, and by one vote, Joe was awarded payment on his own work. He received $10 from each university. This was a lesson for Joe's future: by the time he was 18, he had already learned the difficulties an artist faces in maintaining ownership of his own work.

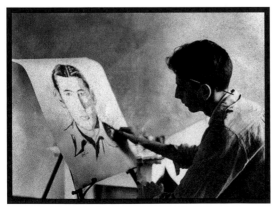

Below: Joe Simon, at age 16, drawing photographer Ralph Amdursky, in Rochester, New York.

Above: Joe Simon, displaying some of his comic book characters.

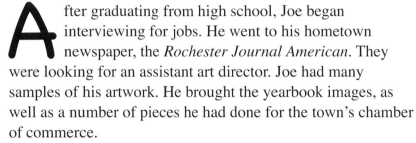

The Newspaper Artist

After graduating from high school, Joe began interviewing for jobs. He went to his hometown newspaper, the *Rochester Journal American*. They were looking for an assistant art director. Joe had many samples of his artwork. He brought the yearbook images, as well as a number of pieces he had done for the town's chamber of commerce.

Joe interviewed with Adolph Edler, an experienced art director. Edler scanned all of the teenager's samples. The older man did not seem impressed. Joe left thinking that there was no way he was getting the job. But he was wrong.

In a few short days, Simon was working for the local newspaper for $15 a week—a good salary for a beginner at that time. However, Joe quickly discovered that he had to work very hard and very quickly for his money. His main job was to retouch photographs, improving their look. He also resized photos to fit in the assigned space in a newspaper layout. It was challenging work, and it had to be done quickly to meet the newspaper's deadlines.

For two years, Simon stayed on the job, learning and becoming a fast, skilled art director. When another opportunity arose, Joe moved on, taking a better job at a newspaper in Syracuse, New York.

However, this was the mid-1930s, during the Great Depression, and radio was becoming very popular. More and more people sat down to listen to Jack Benny and *The Shadow*. Advertisers spent their dollars on the airwaves instead of on newspapers. Much to Joe's dismay, his company was purchased by another newspaper, and he was left without a job. Suddenly, he found himself unemployed.

Below: In this assignment for the *Syracuse Journal American* newspaper, Joe Simon drew boxer Joe Louis knocking out Primo Carnera on June 25, 1935.

Above: Joe Simon, seated, at age 18, with mentor Adolph Edler. They worked together in the early 1930s on the *Rochester Journal American* newspaper in Rochester, New York.

Right: A city kid from the late 1930s sits in a window sill reading a comic book.

Below: Superman made his first appearance in 1938 within the pages of *Action Comics* #1.

Joe packed his car and moved to New York City, looking for work. His skills as a retoucher landed him a part-time job at Paramount Pictures, making photos of famous movie stars look even better. He held the job for several months. It paid well, but this wasn't what Joe wanted to do.

Joe Simon found another job, this time working part-time for *True Story* magazine. He created illustrations for their articles. Art director Harlan Crandall noticed that Joe drew great illustrations even while working *fast*. As Joe pointed out, he learned to be fast while working under tight newspaper deadlines.

Crandall said that Joe should consider working in a fairly new industry: comic books. These cheap, pulp magazines took off in June 1938 when *Action Comics* #1 was published, featuring Superman. Within months, comic books and superheroes had become big business.

Joe didn't need to be told twice about finding more work. Taking his portfolio of samples, Simon headed over to a company called Funnies, Inc.

Owner Lloyd Jacquet explained that he hired writers and artists to make comic books for many different publishers. Jacquet had heard that Joe was a good artist. He sent the young man home with an assignment: a Western. Two days later, Joe turned in his seven-page story. Joe himself felt it wasn't great, but it was done quickly.

When Joe went back four days later, Jacquet was *very* happy to see him. Publisher Martin Goodman (the founder of what would later become Marvel Comics) had seen and liked Joe's work. That could mean *lots* of work for Funnies, Inc.

Joe was sent home to create a 10-page main story. His only directions were that the hero had to wear a mask and had to be able to control fire. A few days later, Joe turned in his pages. He had created a story about Dr. Jack Castle, a doctor exposed to the rays of a mad scientist's machine. Instead of being killed, the hero became The Fiery Mask, whose eyes worked like flame-throwers and whose body gave off intense heat.

Joe's story was published in Martin Goodman's *Daring Mystery Comics* #1, January 1940. It was the start of his life's work. His long-underwear characters (as all superheroes in tights were called) followed a pattern: figure out their special powers, and then create a story where they beat the bad guys.

Joe Simon was only in his mid-twenties, but already he was an experienced comic book professional. He continued looking for steps upward, and in 1940 went to work as editor-in-chief for Fox Publications, which was creating such titles as *The Blue Beetle* and *Mystery Men Comics*. It was here that Joe would meet another writer/artist, one who would soon become his business partner and friend for decades to come.

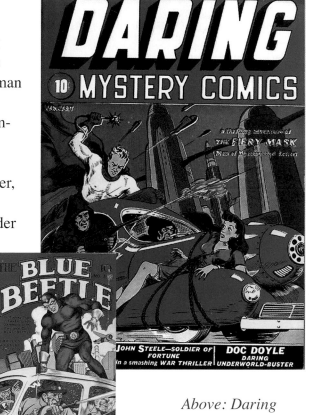

Above: Daring Mystery Comics #1, January 1940, featured the debut of Joe Simon's comic book character, The Fiery Mask. *Above Left: The Blue Beetle* #3, July-August 1940, with cover art by Joe Simon.

Simon & Kirby

Joe began working with Fox's 21-year-old staff artist, Jacob Kurtzberg (who would soon change his name to Jack Kirby). Joe worked on the covers of *Fantastic Comics* and *Mystery Men Comics,* while Jack handled the inside story pages. In May 1940, their first "team" comic books were published.

Joe soon discovered that Jack, like himself, was a fast worker. Jack helped support his parents, and wanted to do additional work in the evenings. Joe had too much to do, and together they began working after-hours on other comic books. It didn't take long for Joe to discover that they would make much more money on their own. Jack was more cautious, but they worked days and nights, creating dozens of comic books for many different publishers.

From their imaginations came *Blue Bolt,* a comic about a college student who is struck by lightning and, with the help of a doctor, gains superhuman strength. But it was another hero, created later that year, who would gain the most fame for Joe Simon and Jack Kirby.

Left: Blue Bolt #1, June 1940, was one of the first Simon and Kirby collaborations. A favorite theme of early comic books was the "woman-in-jeopardy" story, where a strong male hero rescues a damsel in distress. These stories aren't as common today, but the stereotype still lingers.

Above: This 1945 photo, taken during World War II, shows Joe Simon on the right, in his Coast Guard uniform. On the left is his friend and creative partner, Jack Kirby. Standing in the middle is Alfred Harvey, who later went on to start Harvey Comics, publisher of such favorites as *Casper the Friendly Ghost* and *Richie Rich*.

Below: A collection of Simon and Kirby projects created during the 1940s.

Captain America

During the early 1940s, Nazi Germany's Adolf Hitler marched soldiers all across Europe. Around the world, people hated this evil leader. Joe realized that "here was the arch-villain of all time." He needed a hero who could take on and defeat Hitler. So was born *Captain America*.

Joe brought the idea to Martin Goodman (at the time, Goodman's publishing house was called Timely Comics). However, the publisher wasn't sure this was such a great idea. Hitler was hated by millions around the world. The German leader could be dead by the time the comic book was out on newsstands. But Goodman decided to risk it.

With a red, white, and blue costume covering bulging muscles, the heroic figure destined for greatness appeared in the comic book world in December 1940 (although the issue was dated March 1941). Kirby's cover featured Captain America giving Adolf Hitler a knock-out punch to the jaw. Kids across the country were introduced to Joe Simon's character. The weak, mild-mannered Steve Rogers was given a special serum that turned him into the super fighting man whose secret identity as Captain America allowed him to protect the freedom of people in America and around the world.

A million copies were sold, and nearly overnight *Captain America* was a super success! As Joe Simon said, "We were entertaining the world."

Left: Captain America #1.
Facing Page: The opening page of Simon and Kirby's *Captain America #1.*

World War II

I t seemed that everything Joe and Jack did became a success. Many of their titles featured wartime themes, including *All-Winners*, *The Young Allies*, and *Boy Commandos*. They worked for all the major publishers, and even created the first *Captain Marvel* comic for Fawcett Publications.

Writer Bill Parker and artist C. C. Beck had developed the story of Billy Batson, a young radio announcer, who is told by an ancient wizard that by uttering the word "SHAZAM," he could turn into Captain Marvel, the World's Mightiest Mortal. The story character could then battle crime with the combined strengths of the gods: Solomon, Hercules, Atlas, Zeus, Achilles, and Mercury. When the publisher decided to give Captain Marvel his own magazine, the successful team of Simon and Kirby were called in to do the work in record time. However, they were afraid the comic book would fail—they never signed their names to it. That was a mistake—*Captain Marvel* went on to become one of the most successful comic book series ever printed, and Joe and Jack started it all.

Below: A sampling of comic books worked on by the successful team of Joe Simon and Jack Kirby.

Comics were doing great, but the United States was on the edge of war. Finally, on December 7, 1941, Japanese planes attacked the United States naval base at Pearl Harbor, Hawaii. The next day, America declared war on Japan. It was the beginning of World War II.

Joe enlisted in the Coast Guard in 1942. Because he had ridden horses as a hobby, he was assigned to the Mounted Beach Patrol, and was stationed at Barnegat Island, New Jersey. Armed only with a flare gun, his job was to ride up the beach, phone in if everything was OK, then continue patrolling back down the beach. Joe never saw any action during his long, boring year on patrol.

Above: Joe Simon caring for his horse while assigned to the Coast Guard's Mounted Beach Patrol Division on Barnegat Island, New Jersey.

The Art Corps

After his lonely duty with the Mounted Beach Patrol, Joe was assigned to the Coast Guard's Combat Art Corps in Washington, D.C. He was asked to help the war effort by using his comic book skills. He worked on a newspaper comic strip called *True Comics,* which told Coast Guard war stories and tales of the brave sailors who served their country at sea.

After working on the comic strip, Joe suggested to the commander of the Public Information Division that he could further aid the Coast Guard by creating a comic book that centered on the adventures of their heroic soldiers. When it was discovered that comic books sold millions of copies each month, Joe got the OK to go ahead. DC Comics published the comic books. Young and old alike read them. Simon's Coast Guard commander proudly displayed *True Comics*— books that had reached more people than a *New York Times* newspaper article!

Left: Joe Simon and writer Milton Gross' Coast Guard comic, *Adventure is My Career.*

With this success, Joe's *True Comics* began to be published in Sunday comics sections of major newspapers across the country. From this, Joe was asked to produce a comic that would inspire young people to join the Coast Guard. Together with his military friend and newspaper writer, Milton Gross, they created *Adventure is My Career*. Published in 1944, the comic book reached millions of readers, and brought both men a promotion.

In May 1945, Nazi Germany finally surrendered. In August 1945, atomic bombs were dropped on Japan. On September 2, Japan officially surrendered. As Joe would write in his comic strip, *"As wars must, World War Two reaches its end… A victorious America looks to the birth of a new nation."*

Joe was discharged from the Coast Guard, and ready to go back to his job. Luckily, his partner, Jack Kirby, who had been drafted into the Army and fought overseas, had survived the war. By the end of 1945, the daring duo was back in business.

Above: Combat Art Corps illustrators hard at work in the Coast Guard's Washington, D.C., headquarters. Joe Simon sits in the upper left at his drawing board.

Romance

At the offices of Harvey Comics, Joe had met Harriet, the lovely secretary of publisher Alfred Harvey. Joe and Harriet eventually married, and after some long searches in the country, moved into a newly-built home in Mineola, on Long Island, New York. Jack Kirby, his wife Roz, and their daughter moved into a house across the street from the Simons.

Each house had an art studio in the attic. The team worked from home. Sadly, many former comic book artists and writers had died in the war. Simon and Kirby, who had always been busy, now found they had even more creative work to do.

Below: Joe and Harriet Simon on their honeymoon.

New ideas were created all the time. Simon and Kirby realized there was a whole audience of females who wanted comic books. In July 1947, the team came out with *My Date Comics*. It only lasted four issues. Joe and Jack weren't through. They tried again, this time with a comic book about love stories.

In September 1947, *Young Romance* hit the stands. It was a blockbuster.

Published by Prize Comics Group, it quickly became the top romance comic book in the country. All the other comic book publishers came out with copycat titles, but none were as successful as Simon and Kirby's. The comic book was translated into foreign languages and sold throughout the world. It ran for 208 issues, created by many talented people, and finally ended in 1975.

It was the perfect time for success for Joe Simon. He and wife Harriet welcomed their first son, Jon, that same year. Between changing diapers and helping out at home, he and Jack went on to create *Young Love*. Basically, it was the same type of magazine, but with a different title. It resulted in them doubling their income in the romance comic books category. Neither Joe nor Jack complained when more than half the profits went to them, an excellent business deal that Joe had contracted with the publisher. Between the two titles, over two million copies were sold each month!

Of course, Joe and Jack continued working on other titles, including several crime comic books: *Black Cat, Clue, Real Clue Crime,* and *Justice Traps The Guilty.* And then Westerns became popular, with Joe and Jack's *Boys' Ranch* at the top of the list. Jack once said, "It's impossible to tell who did what. We both did everything." They were one of the most popular comic book teams working. Joe believed that it was time to grow further.

Above: Joe Simon holds his four-week-old son, Jon, in 1947.

Left: The Simon and Kirby families, on Long Island, New York, 1945. From left to right: Jack Kirby, daughter Susan, Roz Kirby, Harriet Simon, Joe Simon, and his dog.

Mainline Publications

Simon and Kirby had become the top creative team in comic books. So it was no surprise when, in 1954, Joe and Jack started their own company, Mainline Publications, Inc. Their first comic book was their own creation: *Bullseye, Western Scout*, which came out in May. Shortly thereafter, they also released *Foxhole, In Love*, and *Police Trap*. Wisely, Joe and Jack chose titles that fit in the most popular categories of the time: Westerns, war adventures, romance, and police stories. Unfortunately, their timing was very bad.

In early 1954, several doctors accused the comic book industry of using too much violence. The doctors believed comic books were corrupting young readers. Specifically, horror and crime comics came under fire, but many people blamed *all* comics. On April 21, 1954, just a few weeks before Joe and Jack's first *Bullseye* comic hit the stands, the government opened hearings in Washington, D.C., to determine if comic books caused juvenile delinquency. Several medical professionals stepped forward to argue this wasn't true. But the damage to the comic book business had been done. Parents believed that comics were bad, and this resulted in a huge decrease in sales.

Facing page: An illustration from Mainline Publications' *Bullseye, Western Scout.*
Right: A sampling of comic books produced by Mainline Publications in the 1950s.

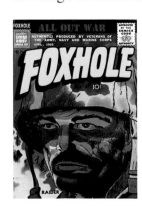

To stop the death of the industry, comic book publishers agreed to follow the 1954 Comics Code Authority (CCA), which called for all comic books to have their seal of approval. Very specific rules were outlined on what would be allowed. Many people thought this violated the First Amendment, the right of free speech, but the comic book industry agreed to this censorship in order to stay in business.

Still, many publishers and printers went out of business. The distributors who sent the comic books to stores across the country also went out of business. Artists, writers, inkers, and letterers were suddenly unemployed. It was a horrible time to be in comics.

Even though their business began with such promise, and even though Joe and Jack followed all the rules set up by the CCA, Mainline went out of business by the end of 1955. As Joe Simon later said, "After the mid-1950s comics crash, it just wasn't fun anymore." Joe decided that it was time to do something different.

Below: Two politicians examine a bulletin board displaying comic books that were judged inappropriate for children to read. Simon and Kirby's *Black Magic* was included on the list of "offensive" comic books.

Above: Urged on by their parents, two children add to a pile of comic books destined for a bonfire to protest offensive stories and illustrations.

Comics and Advertising

Although Joe and Jack continued working in comics, the team began to drift apart. Jack worked on various comic books, taking jobs from the few publishers still in business. Joe went to work for Harvey Comics, taking a job as an idea man. His role was to come up with several ideas for new comics every month. But within a few years, Joe found a whole new area to work in: advertising.

An old friend, Martin Burstein, ran an advertising business. His main clients were people running for government office. Candidates hired the Burstein and Newman advertising and public relations firm to help with their election campaigns. Joe became the art director, creating pamphlets and posters and whatever print materials needed to be produced. But Joe's skills as a comic book artist just couldn't be tucked away.

When millionaire Nelson Rockefeller ran for governor of New York state in 1958, he hired Burstein's company for advertising and publicity. When Rockefeller heard that the famous Joe Simon worked there, the wealthy candidate immediately wanted to do a comic book for his election campaign.

Joe created a comic book biography and a list of the candidate's good deeds. Rockefeller went on to win the election, and Joe's comic book format was used by many of Burstein's other political clients. Not surprisingly, Joe was back in the comic book business once again.

Above: A comic book created by Joe Simon for Nelson Rockefeller's 1958 election campaign for the governorship of New York state.

Sick Magazine

I n 1960, Joe went back to do freelance comic book work for Crestwood Publications, a company he and Jack Kirby had worked for in the 1950s. At first, there was little money in the low-cost comics being made there. Then, owner Teddy Epstein took a look at the amount of money EC Comics' *Mad* magazine was bringing in. The original crazy humor magazine began in 1953, and had become a top-selling title. Epstein wanted some of *Mad's* audience, and asked Joe to come up with a take-off.

Hiring humor writer Dee Causo and several artists, Simon developed *Sick* ("A Grim Collection of Revolting Humor"). The first issue was published in the summer, with an August 1960 date. One of the cover stories was: "Hitler is Still Alive!" Joe Simon slammed the evil German once again, just as when Captain America had punched Hitler in the jaw nearly 20 years earlier.

Facing page: a cover design for *Sick*, with art by Joe Simon. *Below:* Another *Sick* illustration.

Created for older "young adult" readers, the magazine spoofed the people and happenings of the times, creating both fans and foes. It became known for its "*Sick*" jokes. The magazine became very popular, and for eight years Joe continued working on it, owning 50 percent of the profits. However, Crestwood was less successful with other titles. Eventually, Teddy Epstein wanted to sell *Sick* to clear his debts. Luckily, wise businessman Joe Simon still had the original eight-year-old letter, signed by himself and Teddy Epstein, declaring that Simon owned the title. Simon received half the value and continued working with the new owner, Pyramid Books, for another two years. *Sick* changed hands again, but the magazine continued to be published until 1980, with Joe working on it for a number of those years.

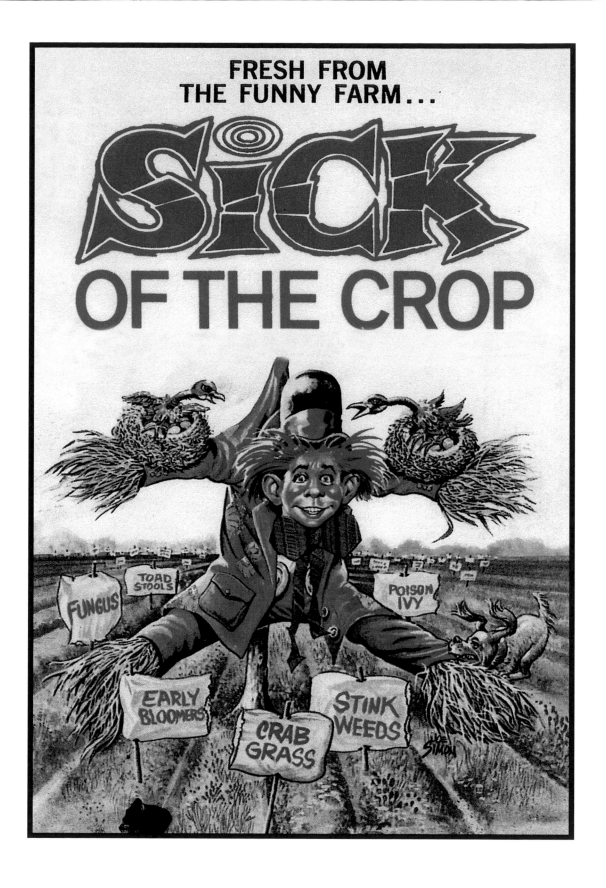

A Proud Artist

Joe Simon continued to work, spending over half a century creating, drawing, and selling comic books. His work, and his partnership with Jack Kirby, has been an inspiration to artists around the world.

In the 1970s, 1980s, and 1990s, many comic book artists and writers were fighting for their rights to the work they had created. For many years, publishers claimed that they owned the creative work, which they had paid for. But by the end of the 20th century, comic book creators—the writers and artists—fought for and won the ownership and money they deserved when one of their creations became a huge hit.

Simon's own business sense helped protect him with *Sick,* and for much of his earlier work. He had learned in his teens, with his yearbook art, how important the business deals really were. However, it took the help of many people, for other artists (including Simon's own partner Jack Kirby) to have their work returned to them. With pressure from comic book

Right: Joe Simon gives a talk about art to a group of kids in an elementary school classroom.

readers, as well as television and radio, many artists finally either got paid for their work or had their original creations returned to them, including Jack Kirby.

As the years passed and the world marked the turn of the century and beyond, the amazing artist and businessman Joe Simon, aged into his 90s, continued to be a rare but popular guest at comic book conventions. He once remarked, "To look back and know that I have had a pivotal role in the development of comics is something I'm very proud of, although it's not something I think about unless someone brings it up."

Amazingly, Captain America lives once again, drawn and written by a new generation of artists and writers. Joe Simon's 1940 creation has come back to fight and protect America in a new era. Few characters have had the power to survive nearly seven decades, and still be read by millions!

Joe Simon's creative mind and talented hands have brought everything from action and adventure, to laughter and fun, to hundreds of millions of readers, young and old, around the world. Joe Simon will forever remain one of the few founders and amazing artists of the comic book industry.

Below: Joe Simon with Captain America, his best-known comic book creation.

Glossary

CENSORSHIP
The control of what is written or spoken by a central authority, often a government or large group of outspoken individuals.

COMICS CODE AUTHORITY (CCA)
Established in 1954 as a way for comic book publishers to deal with parents' concerns about the effects of crime and horror comics on kids. Every comic book published required the CCA's seal of approval, and had to follow a strict set of guidelines. The Code is still in use today, although not all comic books are published with the CCA seal.

CREATOR
A person who thinks up the personality, physical look, and special skills of a comic book character.

GREAT DEPRESSION
A time in America's history, beginning in 1929 and lasting for several years, when the stock market crashed, which resulted in business failures across the country, and the loss of jobs for millions of Americans.

ILLUSTRATE
To add a piece of art to a printed story. The art may be a drawing, painting, or photo.

IMMIGRANTS
People who move from one country to another, taking the new country as their home.

Juvenile Delinquency

A juvenile is a young person, usually under the age of 18. Delinquency means acting antisocially, or breaking the law. In the mid-1950s, many people thought comic books that showed a lot of violence or antisocial behavior caused children to become juvenile delinquents. This debate is being argued again today, with violent video games taking the place of comic books.

Pulp Magazines

A nickname for fiction magazines published on the cheapest possible paper made from wood pulp. Also called "the pulps."

Superheroes

Characters, often human, but they may also be alien or mythological beings, who develop or have special skills that give them superhuman powers. These characters use their powers for good, helping and protecting people.

World War II

A war that was fought from 1939 to 1945, involving countries around the world. The United States entered the war after Japan's bombing of the American naval base at Pearl Harbor, in Oahu, Hawaii, on December 7, 1941.

Above: Joe Simon with a group of fans in Jamaica.

Index